AFTERNOON TEA COOKBOOK

1

SUSAN SAM

TABLE OF CONTENTS

Battenberg Cake

Pineapple Upside Down Cupcakes

Strawberry Cheesecake Bites

Lemon Curd Tarts

Lavender Tea Bread

Macaron I

Mini Chocolate Chip Shortbread Cookies

Lemon Cupcakes

Profiteroles

Victoria Sponge Cake

Mini Dessert Brownies With Raspberries

Rose Petal Cookies

Mini Key Lime Pies

Perfect Lemon Curd

Lavender-Earl Grey Tea Cookies

Easy Scones

Simple Fairy Cakes

Very Quick Sponge Cake

INTRODUCTION

English afternoon tea or simply afternoon tea is generally a traditional blend of teas starting from India, China, Africa and Sri Lanka. Afternoon tea blends in many cases are lighter than breakfast period blends, being designed to "complement, rather than mask the flavor from your afternoon tea meal"

Afternoon Tea is meals made up of sandwiches (usually cut gently in to 'fingers'), scones with clotted cream and jam, nice pastries and cakes. Oddly enough, scones have currently been not a common feature of early Afternoon Tea and were just launched in the 20th century.

1. My Soft Cheese With Chopped Cucumber Afternoon Tea

Ingredients

4 folded flat breads
3 tbls soft cheese
1 mini cucumber diced small

Directions

Combine the cheese and cucumber together.
Butter the flat breads.
Add the soft cheese mix within the flat bread.
Add them to providing plate with cup of tea and serve.

2. My Afternoon Tea Open Scones With Cherry Jam And Clotted Cream

Ingredients

Two scones cut in half buttered makes 4 halves
One tbls jam of your choice on each half
One heaped tbls clotted cream on each half

Directions

Cut and butter the 4 halves scones.
Add a tbls jam on each 50 percent.
Subsequent add the heap tbls of clotted cream on top.
Make a glass of tea and provide the scones with tea.

3. Dainty Cucumber Sandwiches For Afternoon Tea

Ingredients

2 slices thinly cut bread
Butter to spread
0.25 cucumber
Salt and pepper

Directions

Generate your bread and cut the crusts off.
Spread both pieces thinly with butter.
Season both buttered sides with recently ground black pepper and a sprinkle of sea salt (don't skip this step as it's what will lift your sandwich to afternoon tea levels!)
Cut the cucumber in long thin lengths about 2/3 mms heavy.
Enough thickness to keep some turmoil but not enough to make it rustic and large!
Put the two halves together and cut in two, then by 50 percent again lengthways tomorrow make finger sandwiches.

4. My Afternoon Tea I

Ingredients

8 round shape crackers
A few cheese and cranberry to fit on crackers
A few red cheese with spring onion and chives to fit crackers
2 Strawberry soft biscotti fruity cake
4 halves Tomato sliced thin (optional)

Directions

Add the cheeses to the 8 crackers.
Then add the tomatoes to just 4 crackers on top of both different cheeses.
Add the 2 biscotti to both offering dishes.
Add the cup of tea. Offer and enjoy.

5. My Cheesy Tuna On Crackers

Ingredients

0.5 tin tuna chunks
2 heaped tbls soft cheese
Three thickish slices cucumber diced into tiny squares
1 little salt
1 pinch black pepper
0.5 tsp lemon juice (optional)

Directions

Drain the tuna I seriously take good thing about tuna in
drinking water. Help to increase a dish.
Add the soft cheese.
Next cut the cucumber and boost the tuna.
Makes little crunchy pieces in the combine.
Mix well and add the sodium and pepper and lemon juice
incorporate in after that spread on choosing crackers or
toasted bread or inside small pastries.
Serve and luxuriate in.

6.   Anyone For English Afternoon Tea

Ingredients

Scones if thick, slice across the middle and make four portion
1 few butter on each
One tsp strawberry jam on each spread it
One tbls clotted cream on each

Directions

Butter then add the strawberry jam.
Subsequent add the clotted cream on most of the strawberry jam. Then provide having a cup of tea.

7. Apple Cake For Afternoon Tea

Ingredients

3-4 apples, washed, peeled
1 cup (180 g) all-purpose flour
2 tsp baking powder
Pinch salt
2/3 cup (150 g) sugar
2 eggs
0.5 cup (100 ml) milk
1 lemon zest
1/3 cup (60 g) oil
1 tbsp icing sugar to sprinkle on top cake
Fresh double cream, whipped

Directions

Pre-specified the oven to a moderate temperatures 170C (340F) levels.

Clean the apples with solution of just one teaspoon of Bicarbonate Sodium or Soda Bicarbonate blended in warm drinking water. After that force them into a huge cup dish and initiate to peel the skin. Cut into 4 segments then cut each into fifty percent then to cut into 3 parts. Within a huge dish defeat the sugars and eggs with hands then add lemon zest, oil and milk and combine with hands. In another normal size bowl sift the flour, baking natural powder & sodium to prevent the mounds. Add the flour mixture into ovum mixture just a little at the same time and mix with a rubber spatula perfectly.

At this point put the apples pieces into flour mixture and carefully mix completely with the rubberized spatula. Grease a curved baking container with oil or melted butter on the bottom and edges tin, add the flour, and then move off any flour from the container.

Now put the apples mix into the ready cooking tin & smooth top level with large wedding cake spatula. Place in the preheated oven in a middle stand and bake for 30 minutes. Test with a skewer put on top center comes out clean. Remove. Allow it to cool in container for 10 minutes. Release the dessert with a cutter put along the inside edge to divided in the wedding cake.

After that lift away of the container and flip within the cake on a wire to cool. Cake happens to be upside down. Generate an offering plate, flip back again, Add Icing sugar at the top wedding dessert.

To serve on afternoon tea: cut into an area pieces with a dollop of whipped cream or with vanilla your favorite ice cream and a glass of tea.

8. English Tea Cucumber Sandwiches

Ingredients

1 cucumber, peeled and thinly sliced
1 (8 ounce) package cream cheese, softened
0.25 cup mayonnaise
0.25 teaspoon garlic powder
0.25 teaspoon onion salt
1 dash Worcestershire sauce
One (1 pound) loaf sliced bread, crusts removed
1 pinch lemon pepper (Optional)

Directions

Place cucumber slices between 2 paper shower towels emerge a colander. Allow water to drain, about 10 minutes.

Blend cream cheese, mayo, garlic clove natural powder, onion sodium, and Worcestershire spices in a dish until smooth.

Spread cream cheese mix equally on one part of each breads slice.

Separate cucumber slices over fifty percent of the breads slice; sprinkle lemon pepper on cucumber.

Stack the partner of the breads slices spread-side down over cucumber to make sandwiches; cut into triangles.

9. Baby BLT

Ingredients

1 pound bacon, cooked and crumbled
0.5cup mayonnaise
0.25 cup green onions, chopped
2 tablespoons chopped fresh parsley
24 cherry tomatoes

Directions

Place bacon in a huge, deep frying pan. Prepare over medium-high temperature for six to 8 moments, or until equally brownish. Once cooled down, fall apart and set apart.

In a dish, mix together mayo, bacon, green onions, and parsley until well blended. Arranged apart.

Cut a very little slice from the top of every tomato. Using a melon baller or small spoon, scoop inside every tomato and dispose of. Fill each tomato with the bacon combination, and refrigerate intended for one hour. Provide completely chilled.

10. Salmon Wraps

Ingredients

1 (8 ounce) package cream cheese, softened
2 tablespoons chopped fresh dill
2 tablespoons chopped fresh chives
1 tablespoon lemon juice
3 (8 inch) flour tortillas
6 slices smoked salmon

Directions

Combine cream cheese, dill, chives, and lemon juice together in a bowl.
Spread cream cheese on 1/3 of each tortilla. Lay two salmon slices on top; roll strongly and seal edges with a dab of cream cheese. Cut each move into 1-inch sections.

11. World's Best Scones

Ingredients

Scones:
1.75 cups all-purpose flour
4 teaspoons baking powder
0.25 cup white sugar
⅛ teaspoon salt
5 tablespoons unsalted butter
0.5 cup dried currants
0.5 cup milk
0.25 cup sour cream

Egg Wash:
1 egg
1 tablespoon milk

Directions

Pre-specified the oven to 400 degrees Fahrenheit (200 degrees C). Grease a bed sheet pan.

Make the scones: Sift flour, baking powder, blood sugar, and sodium into a considerable bowl. Cut in butter with a pastry food blender or by massaging between fingertips until lumps would be the sizes of peas. Mix in currants.

Beat dairy and bitter cream together in a measuring glass; carefully stir into flour mixture until dough is moistened, being careful not to overwork the dough.

With floured hands, pat dough into two to three inch diameter tennis balls. Place onto the ready sheet skillet and flatten gently. Scones should somewhat touch each other.

Associated with egg clean: Whisk egg and milk together. Clean the tops of scones with egg wash and let them rest for approximately ten minutes.

Bake in the preheated oven until the tops are golden brown, ten to fifteen minutes.

12. Madeleines

Ingredients

2 large eggs
0.5 teaspoon vanilla extract
0.5 teaspoon lemon zest
1 cup confectioners' sugar
0.75 cup all-purpose flour
0.25 teaspoon baking powder
0.5 cup butter, melted and cooled

Directions

Pre-specified the oven to 375 degrees Fahrenheit (190 degrees C).

Grease and flour 24 3-inch madeleine molds.

Beat ovum, vanilla, and lemon zest in a medium bowl with the mixing machine on high speed for 5 moments. Gradually beat in confectioners' sugar.

Beat for five to seven minutes or until thick and satiny.

Sift together flour and cooking powder.

Sort 0.25 from your flour mixture within the egg mixture, softly collapse in.

Collapse in the leftover flour by fourths. After that fold in the melted and cooled down butter. Spoon batter into the ready conforms, filling 0.75 full.

Bake in the preheated oven until the sides are golden and the tops springtime back again, 10 to 12 moments. Cool in conforms around the rack intended for 1 minute. Release cookies with a blade.

Invert cookies on to a rack and let cool.

Sift confectioners' sugars within the covers or dissolve semi-sweet chocolate chips and dip the tips in the chocolate. Store inside an airtight package.

13. Battenberg Cake

Ingredients

1 cup butter, softened
1 cup white sugar
3 eggs
0.25 teaspoon vanilla extract
2 cups all-purpose flour
1 teaspoon baking powder
⅛ teaspoon salt
2 drops red food coloring
1 cup apricot preserves
2 cups ground almonds
3 cups confectioners' sugar
1 egg, room temperature
1.5 teaspoons lemon juice
0.25 teaspoon almond extract

Directions

Preheat oven 350 degrees Fahrenheit (175 degrees C).
Cream butter and just one cup sugar together. Beat in
three eggs, one at a time. Blend vanilla. Blend in flour,
cooking food powder and salt gently. Add dairy products
if needed.

Individual batter into 2 equal parts. Add food coloring to
1 part to generate a deep pink color. Grease two 7 inch
square kitchenware. Spread batters into pans.

Bake at 350 degrees Fahrenheit (175 degrees C) until put
wooden pick comes out clean, about 25 to 50 percent one
hour. Enable stand in kitchenware 5 mins. Turn out on
racks to cool.

Trim edges from both cakes. Cut each wedding cake
lengthwise into 4 strips as wide as the wedding ceremony
wedding cake is thick. Cut to make items match. Heat
your jam slightly. Spread on sides to stuff 2 red and 2
white pieces together checkerboard fashion. Spread all 4
sides of completed cake with your jam. Replicate with
leftover red and white lines. Makes two cakes.

To produce almond paste: Mix almonds, confectioners' sugar, egg, lemon juice, and almond extract together. Rub until easy, adding a bit of lemon juice or water if too dry to move. Add only 0.5 teaspoon every time. It can be stiff. Separate into 2 the same parts.

Roll 0.5 of paste 1/8 inches approximately solid on the top gently dusted with confectioners' sugar. Cut to complement period of wedding cake, and lengthy enough to protect 4 sides leaving ends found out. Lay cake on a single complete of paste. Cover to completely block off all 4 edges of cake pinching insert to seal. Move around in granulated sugars. Place with seal beneath on providing dish, or store in plastic bag. Replicate for second wedding cake. Chill. Cut very finely to provide.

14. Pineapple Upside Down Cupcakes

Ingredients

Cooking spray
0.5 cup butter, melted
1.5 cups brown sugar
24 maraschino cherries
1 (20 ounce) can crushed pineapple
1 (18.25 ounce) package pineapple cake mix
1⅓ cups pineapple juice
⅓ cups vegetable oil
3 eggs
One tablespoon confectioners' sugar for dusting, or as needed

Directions

Pre-specified the oven to 350 degrees Fahrenheit (175 degrees C). Move an oven stand to the middle of the oven. Spray twenty-four muffin cups with cooking spray.

Spoon 1 tsp dissolved butter in to the bottom level of each dispersed muffin cup. Spoon 1 tablespoon brownish glucose into each muffin cup. Press a maraschino cherry in to the center of the brown glucose in each muffin glass. Spoon a heaping tablespoon of smashed pineapple at the top little it with the again of the teaspoon into an amount layer.

Blend pineapple cake blend, pineapple juice, veggie oil, and ovum in a substantial bowl with an electrical mixing machine on low speed until moistened, about 30 seconds. Improve speed to medium; mix for 2 minutes.

Pour combination in to the muffin cups, filling up these to the top; do not overfill.

Cook in the preheated oven until a toothpick inserted into the center of a cupcake comes away clean, about 20 minutes.

Series a work surface with waxed paper. Enable cupcakes to cool at least 5 minutes before inverting muffin mugs on to the waxed paper; serve with pineapple and cherry edges up. Sprinkle cupcakes lightly with confectioners' sugar before providing.

15. Strawberry Cheesecake Bites

Ingredients

1 (8 ounce) package cream cheese
0.5 cup confectioners' sugar
Two teaspoons vanilla extract
12 large fresh strawberries, hulled
Two tablespoons graham cracker crumbs
Two (1 ounce) squares semisweet chocolate chips
(Optional)
1 teaspoon canola oil (Optional)

Directions

Collection a baking sheet with waxed paper.

Beat together the cream cheese, confectioners' glucose, and vanilla extract in a bowl until smooth.

Spoon the combo in a piping bag fitted with a major round tip.

Having a sharp paring knife, cut a cone form aside of the best of each strawberry to leave a little hollow.

Tube about 1 tablespoon of the cream cheese filling up into each strawberry, making sure that the filling overflows a little from the top of the strawberry.

Place the graham cracker breadcrumbs into a shallow bowl. Dip the filled side of the strawberry in to the graham cracker breadcrumbs, coating the uncovered filling with breadcrumbs.

Melt the chocolates and canola essential oil in a microwave-safe cup or ceramic dish in 30-second periods, stirring after every interval, until warm and easy, 1 to 3 mins (depending on your microwave).

Drop the unfilled ends of the strawberries in to the dissolved delicious chocolate and place upon the ready cooking sheet; refrigerate till set.

16. Lemon Curd Tarts

Ingredients

0.25 cup lemon curd
1 (1.9 ounce) container frozen miniature Phyllo Shells, thawed
0.5 cup frozen whipped topping, thawed
0.25 teaspoon ground cinnamon, or to taste

Directions

Spoon about one teaspoon lemon curd to the bottom level of every Phyllo Shell; best with whipped topping. Sprinkle a light dusting of cinnamon inside the best.

17. Lavender Tea Bread

Ingredients

0.75 cup milk
3 tablespoons finely chopped fresh lavender
6 tablespoons butter, softened
1 cup white sugar
2 eggs
2 cups all-purpose flour
1.5 teaspoons baking powder
0.25 teaspoon salt

Directions

Pre-specified the oven to 325 degrees Fahrenheit (165 degrees C). Grease and flour a nine x five inch loaf pan. Combine the milk and lavender in saucepan over medium temperatures. Heat to a simmer, then remove from heat, and permit to cool somewhat.

In a moderate bowl, cream collectively the butter and sugar until clean. Beat in the egg until the mixture is light and cozy. Combine the flour, cooking powder, and sodium; stir into the creamed mix at the same time with the dairy and lavender till just mixed. Put into the ready pan.

Cook to get 50 minutes in the preheated oven, or until a wood pick put in the crown of the loaf comes out clean. Cooling in the frying pan on the cable connection rack.

18. Macaron I

Ingredients

4 extra large egg whites
1 ⅔ cups confectioners' sugar
1 ⅓ cups almond flour
⅛ teaspoon salt
0.25 cup superfine (castor) sugar
0.25 cup seedless raspberry jam

Directions

Place egg whites to a metal combining dish and refrigerate, almost eight hours to right aside.
Remove egg white-colored from the refrigerator and provide to room temp, twenty to 30 a few mins.
Whisk confectioners' blood sugar and almond flour together within a bowl.
Add salt to egg white-colored and defeat with the mixing machine on medium rate till foamy, regarding 1 minute.
Boost the speed to high and steadily beat in superfine blood sugar, about 1 tablespoon at an interval, until egg white are glossy and keep stiff highs, 3-5 more a few of minutes.
Lightly fold almond flour mixture into whipped egg white until thoroughly included. Spoon meringue in to a pastry bag fitted utilizing a 3/8-inch tip. Range two baking sheets with parchment paper.

Tube 1-inch hard disks of meringue two inchs apart on to the prepared cooking sheets; batter will certainly spread. Lift the cooking sheets up a few inchs and drop all of them carefully onto the function surface a number of occasions to remove any sort of air pockets. Allow stand in area temperature till the shiny areas dulls and a slim skin forms, regarding a quarter-hour.

Meanwhile, preheat the oven to 280 levels F (138 levels C). Place the baking sheet in the preheated oven and cook with all the oven door damaged until macaron are completely dried away for the top, concerning a quarter-hour. Remove through the oven and let great totally within the baking sheet, regarding 30 mins or so. Thoroughly peel parchment paper from macaron to remove. Spread 0.5 from the macaron with jam, from then on best with outstanding macaron and press lightly to force jam towards the sides. Refrigerate till macaron soften, two hours to immediately.

19. Mini Chocolate Chip Shortbread Cookies

Ingredients

2 cups all-purpose flour
1 cup butter, softened
0.5 cup confectioners' sugar
1 teaspoon vanilla extract
One (12 ounce) package miniature chocolate chips, divided
1 tablespoon vegetable shortening

Directions

Pre-specified the oven to three hundred and fifty degrees Fahrenheit (175 degrees C).

Combine flour, butter, glucose, and vanilla extract in a dish until dough is smooth. Hold 0.25 the delicious chocolate chips; mix remaining chips into dough till evenly distributed. Move dough into twenty-four small logs make a baking sheet.

Bake in preheated oven until relatively golden around the edges, 15 to 20 minutes. Great in sheet frying pan for a couple of minutes just before removing to great completely on the wire rack.

Break down shortening within a tiny saucepan more than medium-low heat; mix in reserved delicious chocolate chips till melted, about five mins. Drop cookies into scrumptious delicious chocolate and go back again to baking skillet. Refrigerate till firm.

20. Lemon Cupcakes

Ingredients

Cupcakes:
3 cups self-rising flour
0.5 teaspoon salt
1 cup unsalted butter, at room temperature
2 cups white sugar
4 large eggs, at room temperature
2 tablespoons lemon zest
1 teaspoon vanilla extract
1 cup whole milk, divided
2.5 tablespoons fresh lemon juice, divided

Lemon Cream Icing:
2 cups chilled heavy cream
0.75 cup confectioners' sugar
1.5 tablespoons fresh lemon juice

Directions

Pre-specified the oven to 375 degrees Fahrenheit (190 degrees C). Line 30 cupcake pan cups with paper line.
Prepare the cupcakes: Sift flour and sodium together in a bowl. Beat butter and sugar jointly in another dish with an electrical mixer until light and fluffy. Add in eggs one-by-one, beating after every addition to consist of.
Blend lemon zest and vanilla extract.
Lightly beat flour blend into butter blend, 1/3 at a time, switching with 0.5 of the milk and 0.5 through the lemon juice after each of the first two improvements of flour.
Defeat until simply mixed; do not really overmix.
Fill the ready cupcake line with batter, 0.75 full, and cook in the preheated oven until a toothpick inserted in the middle comes away clean, regarding seventeen minutes.
Allow the cupcakes cool in the pans prior to removing these to complete cooling upon the rack, regarding a couple of minutes.

In the meantime, connected with topping: Defeat cream within a chilled dish with an electric mixing machine set on low until cream begins to thicken. Add confectioners' sugars and lemon juice, a little at any kind of given time, defeating after each addition, until completely integrated. Increase the mixing machine speed to high and defeat till the topping forms soft highs, regarding 5 mins.

Spread icing on cooled down cupcakes.

Refrigerate left over spots.

21. Profiteroles

Ingredients

1 cup water
0.5 cup butter
0.25 teaspoon salt
1 cup all-purpose flour
4 eggs
1 cup heavy cream
0.25 cup confectioners' sugar
1 teaspoon rose water (Optional)
1 cup heavy cream
9 ounces semisweet chocolate, chopped

Directions

Pre-specified the oven to 425 levels Fahrenheit (220 levels C). Line a sheet pan with parchment paper.

Accept the water to a boil within a saucepan. Stir in the butter and salt until the butter has blended; take away the saucepan from the warmness. Stir in the flour until just no dry mounds stay; stir in the eggs, one-by-one, adding the following egg only following a last one provides been completely built-in in to the mixture. Drop the profiterole paste upon to the ready sheet pan in equally spaced dollops.

Cook in the preheated oven till the pastries possess puffed up and switched golden brownish, 25 to 30 moments. Remove from your cooking sheet pan and cool upon a cable stand to space heat.

Beat 1 glass of weighty cream to smooth highs; stir in the confectioners' sugars and rosewater till the sugar offers blended. Accept the remaining cup of large cream to a simmer in a little saucepan more than moderate heat. Remove from the warmth and stir in the chocolate till dissolved and easy.

To construct, stick an opening in to the bottom level of each pastry and fill with the rose drinking water cream. Place the filled profiteroles upon to individual providing dishes and best with the warm spices. Leftover profiteroles may be saved protected inside an airtight container in the refrigerator up to 5 days.

22. Victoria Sponge Cake

Ingredients

1 cup all-purpose flour
1.5 teaspoons baking powder
1 cup butter, softened
1 cup confectioners' sugar
2 large eggs, room temperature
1 teaspoon vanilla extract
0.5 cup milk, room temperature

Directions

Pre-specified the oven to 400 degrees Fahrenheit (200 degrees C).
Grease an 8-inch springform pan.
Sift flour and food preparation powder into a medium bowl make aside.
Defeat butter and glucose with the mixing machine until light and fluffy. The mix should be significantly lighter in color. Add eggs one-by-one, allowing each egg to blend in to butter mix before adding the following. Beat in vanilla.
Add flour blend in amounts, switching with dairy, blending batter quickly after each addition in order to combine
Pour mix into the ready pan.
Bake in the preheated oven until a toothpick inserted in the middle comes away clean, about 20 minutes. Cool the cake in the pan for 10 minutes, then change the cake away onto a cable connection rack to great completely.

23. Mini Dessert Brownies With Raspberries

Ingredients

2 teaspoons butter
2 teaspoons all-purpose flour
1 cup butter
1.5 cups white sugar
4 eggs, lightly beaten
2 teaspoons vanilla extract
1 cup all-purpose flour
⅔ cup unsweetened cocoa powder
0.5 teaspoon baking powder
0.25 teaspoon salt

Ganache:
⅓ cup heavy cream
3 ounces bittersweet chocolate, finely chopped

Topping:
28 fresh raspberries

Directions

Pre-specified the oven to three hundred and fifty degrees Fahrenheit (175 degrees C).
Oil and flour a 12-cup mini muffin pan and an 8-inch square skillet with 1 teaspoon butter and 1 teaspoon flour every.
Melt 1 glass butter in a major saucepan more than moderate heat. Remove from heat; mix in sugar, ovum, and vanilla extract till smooth. Collapse in an one glass flour, cacao natural powder, cooking powder, and sodium gently.
Spoon batter into the prepared muffin cups using a little snow cream scoop, filling up each 0.75 complete. Pour outstanding mixture into the rectangular pan.

Cook both pans in the preheated oven till a toothpick placed into the middle comes out with merely a number of crumbs attached, about 12 instances for the mini muffins and 20 minutes for the square pan. Remove from oven and cool in the pan for five minutes.

Transfer rounded brownies to a wire rack to cool. Let 8-inch pan of brownies cool in the pan, about two hours. Cut in to 16 small parts.

Heat cream inside a little saucepan a lot more than medium high temperature till it nearly comes, about several moments.

Place sliced chocolates into a dish. Pour hot cream over delicious chocolate and whisk till easy. Cool till thickened, about two hours.

Create a scrap of ganache onto each brownie piece.

Top every with 1 raspberry.

24. Rose Petal Cookies

Ingredients

14 tablespoons white sugar
12 tablespoons unsalted butter, softened
2 eggs
0.5 teaspoon rose water
1.5 tablespoons dried rose petals
2.5 cups all-purpose flour
1 teaspoon baking powder
1 pinch salt

Directions

Combine sugar and butter in a substantial dish. Beat with the mixer till light and comfortable, regarding 5 minutes. Defeat in ovum and rose drinking water. Mix in went up padding.

Combine flour, cooking powder, and sodium within an individual bowl. Blend in towards the dough. Cover and chill dough to get at least a single hour, or overnight.

Preheat the oven to 400 levels F (200 levels C).

Line baking pan with parchment paper.

Transfer dough on the gently floured surface to regarding 1/3-inch width. Cut into styles utilizing a shaped cutter machine, or maybe cut in to rectangles or pieces. Place cookies 1 inch apart upon the prepared baking sheet.

Bake in the preheated oven till light and sharp, six to 8 minutes. Cool totally before providing.

25. Mini Key Lime Pies

Ingredients

12 mini graham cracker crusts
3 cups sweetened condensed milk
1 cup sour cream
1 cup freshly squeezed key lime juice
3 tablespoons grated key lime zest
2 fresh key limes, thinly sliced
1 (7 ounce) can whipped cream topping

Directions

Pre-specified the oven to three hundred and fifty degrees Fahrenheit (175 degrees C).

Place mini graham cracker crusts on to a baking sheet. In a dish, beat together the sweetened condensed dairy, bitter cream, lime green juice, and lime green zest till easy. Pour the filling up in the graham cracker crusts, filling up to the best.

Cook in the preheated oven till sizzling, 5 to eight minutes. Refrigerate till thoroughly perfectly chilled, in least 1 hour. To provide, ornament each mini pie with a lime cut and a scrap of whipped cream topping.

26. Perfect Lemon Curd

Ingredients

0.75 cup fresh lemon juice
0.75 cup white sugar
0.5 cup unsalted butter, cubed
3 large eggs
1 tablespoon grated lemon zest

Directions

Combine lemon juice, blood sugar, butter, eggs, and lemon zest in an exceedingly 2-quart saucepan. Prepare over medium-low high temperature, whisking continuously, till mixture thickens and bubbles, regarding six to 7 a few minutes.

27. Lavender-Earl Grey Tea Cookies

Ingredients

1 Earl Grey tea bag
⅓ cup hot milk
0.75 cup white sugar
0.5 cup softened butter
1 egg
1.75 cups all-purpose flour
1 teaspoon baking powder
0.25 teaspoon baking soda
2 teaspoons dried lavender

Glaze:
1 tablespoon lemon juice
1 tablespoon water
0.25 cup white sugar
1 tablespoon dried lavender
1 teaspoon lemon zest

Directions

Pre-specified the oven to 350 degrees Fahrenheit (175 degrees C).

Steep Earl Grey tea bag in hot milk within a bowl.

Blend glucose and butter collectively in a large bowl. Mix in egg. Remove tea bag from tantalizing milk; add milky tea mixture to batter. Add flour, baking powder, food preparation soda, and lavender; mix dough until well combined.

Drop dough by curled spoonfuls onto ungreased cookie sheets.

Prepare in the preheated oven until edges are light brown and place, 10 to 12 mins. Allow cool several of minutes. Whilst cookies are cooking meals, stir lemon juice and water along within a small dish. Add glucose, lavender, and lemon zest and mix till combined. Clean or spoon glaze over on to cooled down cookies.

28. Easy Scones

Ingredients

8oz self-rising flour
Pinch of salt
1 teaspoon of baking powder
2oz softened butter
1oz sugar
1 teacup of milk

Directions

The oven should end up being pre-heated to 200°C when you prepare the mixture. Enable in least two scones per person, more if the guests have big appetites. The amounts the following make 12 scones.
Measure 8oz self-rising flour and add a pinch of salt and a teaspoon of baking organic powder. Using self-rising flour since well as cooking powdered will make your scones rise attractively.
Add 2oz melted butter and 1oz sugar and incorporate to a dough with regarding 1 teacup of dairy. Ends up your dough to a thickness of around half an inches and make use of a cutter of around 2" size to cut in to models. Place upon a greased cooking sheet and prepare for about 12 minutes until well-risen and golden.

29. Simple Fairy Cakes

Ingredients

4oz self-rising flour
4oz margarine
4oz caster sugar
2 eggs

Directions

To get a chocolate variation, remove one tablespoon through the flour and substitute it having a tablespoon of cacao powder. Beat the constituents well, preferably using the combining machine until the mix turns light in color. Collection a 12-hole cupcake container with paper circumstances and separate the mixture similarly among the instances: features out about one dessert teaspoon per wedding cake. Cook at 150°C to get regarding 20 mins. To tell in the event that the cakes are prepared, take every 1 of them from the oven and give consideration carefully to any or all of these: in the event that they are not really ready you will certainly hear a silent bubbling sound. Enable the fairy cake to great upon the cable stand before topping.

30. Very Quick Sponge Cake

Ingredients

8oz flour
8oz margarine
8oz caster sugar
4 eggs

Directions

A simple fail-safe ceremony cake could become created by mixing together 8oz flour. And also caster sugars and margarine, along with 4 ovum. Beat well to get two occasions till the blend becomes pale from then on separate the blend among two greased meal tins. Cook to get approximately 30 mins at 150°C till the cake learn to arrive away from the medial part from the container. Remove from your oven and enable to cool to get some occasions prior to turning away.

Made in United States
Troutdale, OR
08/28/2024

22404030R00035